Street Bikes

Rachel Eagen

CRABTREE PUBLISHING COMPANY
www.crabtreebooks.com

Crabtree Publishing Company
www.crabtreebooks.com

For my talented Special Projects comrades

Coordinating editor: Ellen Rodger
Project Editor: L. Michelle Nielsen
Editors: Carrie Gleason, Adrianna Morganelli, Jennifer Lackey
Design and production coordinator: Rosie Gowsell
Cover design, and production assistance: Samara Parent
Art direction: Rob MacGregor
Scanning technician: Arlene Arch-Wilson
Photo research: Allison Napier
Prepress technician: Nancy Johnson

Consultants: Petrina Gentile Zucco, Automotive Journalist, The Globe and Mail.

Photo Credits: Anthony Collins/Alamy: p. 19 (top); Patrick Eden/Alamy: p. 11; Bernie Epstein/Alamy: p. 9 (top); Geldi/Alamy: p. 16 (bottom); Geomphotography/Alamy: p. 15 (middle); www.gerardbrown.co.uk/Alamy: p. 5 (bottom), p. 12; Martyn Goddard/Alamy: p. 13 (top); Martin Jenkinson/Alamy: p. 29; Motoring Picture Library/Alamy: p. 14 (bottom); Photofusion Picture Library/Alamy: p. 22; Profimedia International s.r.o./Alamy: p. 23 (top); Jiri Rezac/Alamy: p. 17 (top); Alan Stone/Alamy: p. 19 (bottom); SuperStock/Alamy: p. 23 (bottom); Transtock Inc./Alamy: p. 13 (bottom); Vintage Images/Alamy: p. 7 (top);

AP Photo/Morry Gash: p. 30 (bottom); AP Photo/The Oklahoman, Jim Beckel: p. 17 (bottom);
AP Photo/Worcester Telegram & Gazette, Paula Ferazzi Swift: p. 25 (top); Bettmann/Corbis: p. 8, p. 25 (bottom), p. 30 (top); Markus Cuff/Corbis: p. 15 (top); Chris Farina/Corbis: p. 31 (bottom); Ed Kashi/Corbis: p. 27; Lake County Museum/Corbis: p. 6 (top); Reuters/Corbis: p. 4; John Springer Collection/Corbis: p. 10 (top); RICK WILKING/Reuters/Corbis: p. 1; Patrick Ward/Corbis: p. 24, p. 26; Julie Fishe/Getty Images: p. 16 (top); Scherl/SV-Bilderdienst/The Image Works: p. 7 (bottom); Topham/The Image Works: p. 6 (bottom); Ron Kimball/Ron Kimball Stock: cover, p. 5 (top), p. 9 (bottom), p. 10 (bottom), p. 14 (top), p. 15 (bottom), pp. 20-21; Michael Litcher Photography: p. 31 (top); Reuters/ADAC: p. 28.

Illustrations: www.mikecarterstudio.com: p.18

Cover: Some motorcycle shops specialize in making custom bikes, such as this chopper, complete with a custom paint job.

Title page: A motorcyclist rides his low rider bike through the streets of Daytona Beach, Florida during Bike Week, a ten-day event that attracts thousands of motorcycle enthusiasts.

Library and Archives Canada Cataloguing in Publication

Eagen, Rachel, 1979-
    Street bikes / Rachel Eagen.

(Automania!)
Includes index.
ISBN 978-0-7787-3014-9 (bound)
ISBN 978-0-7787-3036-1 (pbk.)

    1. Motorcycles--Juvenile literature. I. Title. II. Series.

TL440.15.E23 2007   629.227'5   C2007-900648-5

Library of Congress Cataloging-in-Publication Data

Eagen, Rachel.
    Street bikes / written by Rachel Eagen.
       p. cm. -- (Automania!)
    Includes index.
    ISBN-13: 978-0-7787-3014-9 (rlb)
    ISBN-10: 0-7787-3014-X (rlb)
    ISBN-13: 978-0-7787-3036-1 (pb)
    ISBN-10: 0-7787-3036-0 (pb)
    1. Motorcycles--Juvenile literature. I. Title. II. Series.

TL440.15.E24 2007
629.227'5--dc22

2007002918

Crabtree Publishing Company

www.crabtreebooks.com   1-800-387-7650

Published in Canada
Crabtree Publishing
616 Welland Ave.
St. Catharines, ON
L2M 5V6

Published in the United States
Crabtree Publishing
PMB16A
350 Fifth Ave., Suite 3308
New York, NY 10118

Published in the United Kingdom
Crabtree Publishing
White Cross Mills
High Town, Lancaster
LA1 4XS

Published in Australia
Crabtree Publishing
386 Mt. Alexander Rd.
Ascot Vale (Melbourne)
VIC 3032

Contents

Born to be Wild

Motorcycles are popular all over the world. They are practical vehicles for getting around in crowded cities. They can also be fun to drive long distances. A street bike is a motorcycle that riders use on regular roads, rather than racing at tracks or taking off-road.

Thrill of the Open Road

People like motorcycles because they are fun to ride. Unlike a car, motorcycles do not have windows or doors, allowing riders to experience the thrill of the open road in an exciting way. Motorcyclists feel the wind whip around their bodies as they accelerate. They also experience the weight of the bike shifting beneath them on corners. Driving a motorcycle is demanding. Riders must learn to shift gears, adjust their riding positions, and remain alert at all times for traffic signals and obstacles in the road. Most motorcyclists want to progress to more complicated and powerful bikes. This challenges them to fine-tune their driving skills so they can become better riders. Many motorcyclists are addicted to this pursuit.

Motorcyclists gathered in 2003 to celebrate the 100th anniversary of Harley-Davidson, a motorcycle company famous worldwide. These riders are in Barcelona, Spain.

4

Custom bikes, or bikes made to suit certain riders, are often one of a kind with a style all their own.

Fun, Yet Practical

Motorcycles have not always had a good reputation because some people view them as being more dangerous than other vehicles. They do not offer the same amount of protection as cars or trucks because they do not have an outer body to keep riders safe in collisions. When driven safely by trained riders, motorcycles have several advantages over larger vehicles. They are **fuel-efficient**. Motorcylces can fill up at a gas station for a fraction of the cost of cars, and their lighter weight means they burn less fuel. Fuel efficiency is also better for the environment, because fewer polluting **emissions** are spouted into the air. Their smaller size means they are easier to park than cars, making them practical in crowded cities. They are also usually less expensive to purchase and maintain than cars.

Styles on the Street

There are many types of street bikes. Dual-sport bikes are motorcycles that have some off-road capabilities, and **handle** easily, making them excellent bikes for beginners. Traditionally, custom bikes were motorcycles that had been modified, or changed, from the original factory version, usually by the bike owners themselves. Many manufacturers now offer their own custom bikes, so that riders have little to do to them after they purchase the bikes from dealerships. Cruisers are large, powerful bikes built for speed and top performance. Performance refers to how well a bike accelerates, decelerates, handles turns, and adjusts to bumps in the road. Riders are interested in performance because it relates to how safe the bike will be on the road.

This touring motorcycle is made by BMW. Touring motorcycles often have two seats and are designed so riders can travel long distances in comfort.

Early Bikes

The first motorcycles appeared in the late 1800s, and were basically bicycles that had small engines strapped to them. Early motorcycles were called "bone shakers" because they did not have suspensions, which cushions riders from bumps in the road.

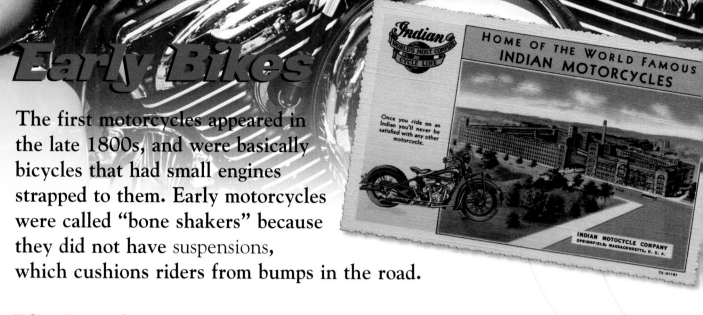

Bike Experiments

Sylvester Howard Roper, from Massachusetts, built one of the first motorized bicycles in 1867. The bike was powered by a **steam engine**. German inventor Gottlieb Daimler built another early version of the motorcycle in 1885 that had a gasoline-powered engine and a body made mostly of wood. It had four wheels: one in the front, one in the back, and two small wheels on either side. Two American companies that specialized in building motorcycles formed in the early 1900s. They were the Indian Motorcycle Company and Harley-Davidson Motor Company.

The War Years

In 1914, World War I, a global conflict that lasted until 1918, broke out in Europe, and the effects of it were felt all over the world. Militaries used motorcycles as messenger vehicles, and sometimes even as ambulances. They were also used to transport supplies, such as guns and ammunition, to soldiers. Motorcycles were faster and more agile than large, bulky tanks, which is what made them so practical during the war. Some motorcycles were even built with special sidecars with machine guns mounted to the body of the sidecar.

(above) This advertisement for the Indian Motorcycle Company shows their factory in Springfield, Massachusetts.

(left) These men were messengers that rode motorcycles through war-torn Europe.

Postwar

After the war ended in 1918, the global **economy** suffered, causing widespread poverty, as many people struggled to find jobs in order to support themselves and their families. The invention of Henry Ford's Model T car, produced from 1908 to 1927, was an **economical**, convenient vehicle that changed the way people thought about transportation. Unlike the vehicles that had come before, the Model T was affordable to most Americans. It was a practical vehicle, allowing people to work farther away from their homes, and offering entire families an opportunity to hop into their cars and go somewhere. Motorcycles were far from the minds of most people at this time, as they could not accommodate more than one person.

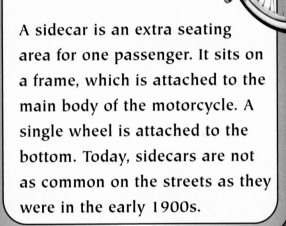

A sidecar is an extra seating area for one passenger. It sits on a frame, which is attached to the main body of the motorcycle. A single wheel is attached to the bottom. Today, sidecars are not as common on the streets as they were in the early 1900s.

Bikes on the Upswing

Motorcycles could have easily disappeared if manufacturers forced them to compete with cars as practical modes of transportation. Instead, motorcycle manufacturers began to promote motorcycle racing, which kept motorcycles in the public eye. Motorcycles were raced among **enthusiasts** from the first days of development. As racing was promoted as a sport, people began to think of motorcycling as a leisure activity, rather than as an alternative to cars. This allowed motorcycles to hang on a little longer.

When motorcycles became popular they were used by messengers and police officers. This policeman is transporting a prisoner.

Picking Up Speed

Motorcycling survived until World War II. Military equipment, such as planes and tanks, were assembled at factories that had once produced cars. Some motorcycle companies produced motorcycles for militaries to use, as they had during World War I. The making of military equipment allowed for some breakthroughs in technology, which were adapted for motorcycles after the war.

Hollywood movies in the 1950s, including The Wild One, *starring Marlon Brando (above), helped to make motorcycles more popular.*

Glory Days

Once World War II was over, the United States and other countries enjoyed a **postwar boom**. The economy improved, and people had money to spend on larger homes, as well as on other luxury items, such as cars. New roads were built, and long highway systems stretched from one end of the country to the other, giving people more reason than ever to go exploring.

Stalling at the Start

People slowly began to consider motorcycles as a mode of transportation rather than as a sport. Hollywood movies in the 1950s and 1960s helped to popularize motorcycles, but were in part responsible for giving motorcyclists a poor reputation, portraying them as **outlaws**. Motorcycles posed other problems. Riders had to kick-start them, or stomp down on a lever with their foot, which required strong legs. They also broke down often and required special care, so riders had to have the mechanical know-how to keep them running.

A Nice Ride

After the war, Japanese manufacturers began making large-sized mopeds, which are small versions of motorcycles that run on less powerful engines. They were meant for everyday transportation, and caught on quickly because heavy city traffic in Japan made cars impractical. Many Japanese motorcycles had electric starters by the late 1950s, which meant they did not have to be kick-started. This **revolutionized** bike technology, as most manufacturers began building bikes with electric starters. In 1961, Honda launched an advertisement campaign called "You meet the nicest people on a Honda." The ads featured everyday people riding Honda motorcycles. This challenged the image of the outlaw biker, and improved the reputation of motorcycles.

Playing Catch-Up

It took a while for other motorcycle manufacturers to catch up with Japanese technology. German manufacturer BMW made excellent bikes in the 1960s and 1970s, but they were expensive and not heavily advertised in the United States, so they did not sell well there. Harley-Davidson could not compete with Japanese manufacturers until it introduced the Evolution, or Evo, engine in 1984. The engine was the most reliable one Harley-Davidson had ever produced, which meant that riders did not have to worry about their bikes breaking down. The Evo helped American street bikes make a serious comeback.

In the 1960s, small, reliable motorcycles made by Japanese manufacturers, including Honda (above), Kawasaki, Suzuki, and Yamaha, started to become popular with American riders.

British manufacturer Triumph became more popular after its 1950 Thunderbird 6T appeared in the movie The Wild One. The Triumph T100SS (below) was built in the early 1960s.

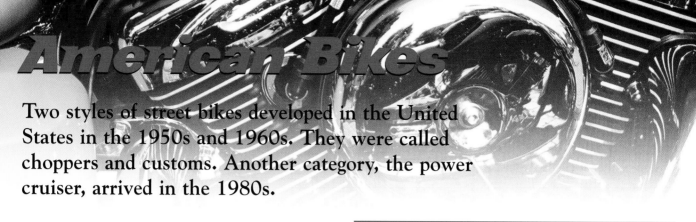

American Bikes

Two styles of street bikes developed in the United States in the 1950s and 1960s. They were called choppers and customs. Another category, the power cruiser, arrived in the 1980s.

Choppers

Choppers first appeared after World War II, when people began exploring the United States on its newly paved highways. Some Harley-Davidson owners customized, or modified, their bikes so they would be more lightweight and could go faster. This often involved "chopping," or removing, parts the owners considered unnecessary, including fenders, lights, front brakes, and anything else that could be removed without making the bikes illegal for street riding. Many Harley-Davidson choppers of the 1960s had high, or "ape-hanger," handlebars, extended forks, and seats that made riders sit back while driving. Choppers continue to be popular today, but many are made in factories, so riders do not have to modify the bikes themselves.

Easy Rider, a movie made in 1969, featured actors Dennis Hopper, Peter Fonda, and Jack Nicholson. It helped make choppers popular.

This chopper was made in 2004. It was modeled after one of the choppers in the movie Easy Rider.

Customs

At one time, customizing meant personalizing a bike or changing it to make it different from the production model, or the one made at the factory. Customizing changed in the 1970s, when bike manufacturers began producing custom bikes in factories. One of the first factory-produced custom bikes was the Super Glide, introduced by Harley-Davidson in 1971. It was made by combining the chopper-like forks of the Sportster model with the frame and powerful engine of the Electra Glide model. By this point, chopping, or bike customizing, was for style. Bikers originally chopped their bikes so they would go faster, but the factory-produced choppers were made to imitate the chopper style. These bikes performed well, but their styling is what made them sell.

Power Cruisers

By the early 1980s, motorcyclists began demanding better performance from their bikes. Sportbikes, which were modeled after racing bikes that had excellent performance and speed, were becoming more popular. Street motorcyclists were looking for performance similar to that of sport bikes in their own bikes, without having to sacrifice the comfort of a street bike. Manufacturers began producing power cruisers, which are powerful street bikes with excellent performance. Harley-Davidson produces some of the best power cruisers today, but other manufacturers worldwide have contributed popular models as well. Power cruisers tend to be more expensive, but for many riders, performance outweighs the cost of these amazing machines.

Rocket III, made by British manufacturer Triumph, is one of the most powerful power cruisers on the road today. It has classic cruiser styling with low handlebars and chrome detailing.

A Comfortable Ride

Dual-sport bikes and touring bikes are very different from each other, but they both offer a comfortable ride. Dual-sport bikes are especially suited to beginning bikers, while tourers are more suited to people who have a lot of biking experience, and are ready to take long trips on their bikes.

Dual-sport Bikes

Dual-sport bikes, which are sometimes called dual-purpose bikes, are street bikes that have some off-road characteristics. This makes them sportier than most street bikes on the road. Most dual-sport bikes have tires with excellent traction, or the ability to grip uneven or dirt surfaces. Dual-sport bikes also feature long-travel suspensions, which cushion riders from large bumps because they allow the bike to pop up and sink down easily. This makes dual-sport bikes ideal for off-road traveling. Dual-sport bikes are lightweight, and they are known for handling well. Both of these qualities make them ideal for new bikers.

Tourers

Touring bikes are large street bikes made to travel long distances. They are built for comfort and **endurance**, allowing riders to travel for hours at a time. They usually accommodate more than one rider. Touring bikes have fairings, which are clear, plastic shields mounted to the front of a bike, and lockable luggage compartments for travelers who require space for extra clothing and supplies. Harley-Davidson is thought to have started the tourer trend when it introduced a fairing and luggage option on its Electra Glide model in the 1960s. Since then, many manufacturers have debuted touring bikes, including Honda's Gold Wing series and the K1200 from BMW.

Fairings are meant to protect riders from rain, snow, and the backsplash of other vehicles.

Sport-tourers

Sport-touring bikes are similar to touring bikes, but are more lightweight, and have the agility and superior handling of sport bikes. Sport-tourers provide more comfortable seating than sport bikes, making them ideal for long-distance travel. Kawasaki introduced the first Japanese sport-tourer with its Concours model in 1986. It was so successful that it changed very little in its first 20 years. The ST1100 from Honda has been another popular sport-tourer, that has been made since 1990. It has a 28-liter fuel tank, making it one of the largest on any street bike. This allows riders to go about 300 miles (480 kilometers) before having to refuel. Smaller fuel tanks of about 4 gallons (15 liters), which are often on sport-tourers, allow bikes to go less than 200 miles (322 kilometers).

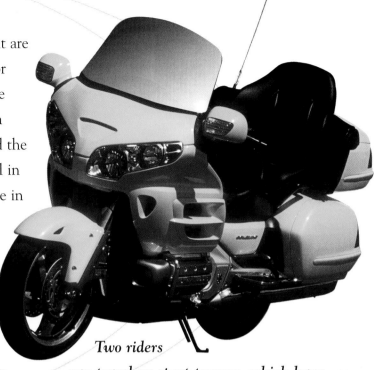

Two riders can travel on sport-tourers, which have large fairings and storage compartments.

Touring cruisers have large-capacity fuel tanks and high-displacement engines, like other touring bikes, making them excellent long-distance rides.

Touring Cruisers

Touring cruiser bikes are also suitable for traveling long distances. They feature passenger comforts, such as windshields and luggage compartments. Touring cruisers differ from touring bikes because they are styled to look like cruisers, with metallic finishes, chrome accents, and an overall tough appearance. Yamaha's Royal Star Venture is a touring cruiser. It is a high performance bike capable of fast speeds, and it has the endurance to travel for long periods of time. The Venture is equipped with **cruise control**, as well as radio speakers. American manufacturer Victory makes the Victory Touring Cruiser. This bike features cushioned floorboards for the driver and passenger, as well as a specially designed suspension to provide a smooth ride over long distances.

Custom Bikes

Many motorcyclists are fascinated by custom bikes, or bikes that have been altered to suit personal taste. The customizing trend, which began in the 1950s, has evolved dramatically over time. Custom bikes are among the most outrageous vehicles on the streets today.

Ride in Style

Customizing took off in the United States after World War II, when riders began removing parts on their bikes to make them lighter, so they would go faster. As technology improved, bikes were made to handle better, with more durable, reliable engines and sleeker frames. Improved performance made customizing unnecessary, but the trend stuck because some people still wanted their bikes to look different from other bikes on the street. Customizing became more geared toward style rather than performance.

Often times, what makes a custom bike so spectacular is its paint job. Skulls and flames are popular images to paint on motorcycles but it is up to each rider.

This Harley-Davidson motorcycle was customized using a sleek design.

A Custom Chop ▶

The first customized bikes in the United States were the choppers of the 1950s and 1960s. The style, which started when bikers began removing weight from their bikes in order to make them go faster, is now geared toward appearance rather than performance. Choppers usually have extended forks and high handlebars, known as "ape hangers," a style that is appealing to some bikers, even though it can make steering difficult. Some choppers have tall, skinny tires on the front and lower, fatter tires on the back, with a seat that allows the rider to lean back while driving.

Low Riders ▶

In 1977, Harley-Davidson introduced its Low Rider, the company's first production, or factory, custom bike. The Low Rider had similar styling to the choppers of the time, but was slightly different. It had lower handlebars and mag wheels, which are made of magnesium alloy, a type of metal. Mag wheels are more lightweight than regular wheels, making bikes more agile. The Low Rider also had attractive chrome-accented body detailing, and featured a low seat. The model was immediately popular.

Long forks are design details of choppers.

15

Café Racers

While the chopper style became popular in the United States during the 1950s and 1960s, a different styling trend took place in Europe, especially in Britain and in parts of Italy. While motorcycling was thought of as an activity for rebels and reckless youths in the United States, people in Europe saw motorcycling as a practical mode of transportation in heavy city traffic. Motorcyclists were more interested in improving the performance of their bikes. This interest in performance inspired motorcyclists to customize their bikes after European racing bikes of the time. Motorcyclists lowered their handlebars and moved the footpegs toward the back of the bike. This made riders lean forward in a crouched position. These bikes became known as café racers. A big part of the café racer scene, aside from riding around on café racer bikes, was listening to rock n' roll and strutting around in studded, black leather jackets and racing goggles, outfits that attracted attention.

Café racers earned their name because the owners were often seen racing from one café to the next, so they would be seen by the young, trendy crowd of the day.

Café racers were nearly flat from front to back, featuring lightweight bodies and powerful engines. The frame of this racer was made by Norton, a British manufacturer that specialized in racing bikes.

Streetfighters

In the 1980s, a new trend of motorcycle customizing developed in Italy, and soon spread to the rest of Europe. These bikes, called streetfighters, were modified sport bikes, or motorcycles that were raced at tracks. At this time, **insurance companies** refused to pay for repairs on expensive sport bikes that were damaged after their owners crashed them at races. Some motorcyclists got their hands on these damaged bikes and customized them for the streets. Plastic body parts were thrown away, as were parts that were not necessary, such as fairings. They replaced only the parts needed to make the bikes street legal, such as headlights. Streetfighters were then painted with **matte** black paint. Streetfighters were lean, mean bikes that looked similar to racing bikes, which appealed to many European motorcyclists in the 1980s.

Originally, streetfighters looked like racing bikes, with few, if any, shiny chrome parts and black paint. Today, they still resemble racing bikes, but many have colorful paint jobs.

Fighting the Streets Today

Streetfighters are popular all over the world today. Some manufacturers started to produce factory versions of streetfighters, although many owners prefer to customize their bikes themselves. Many modern streetfighters start out as race replicas, or motorcycles that are styled after racing bikes, but are more suited to driving on the street. Most streetfighters feature loud exhaust systems, which bike owners customize on their own. Streetfighters also often feature eye-catching paint jobs rather than the matte black paint of the original streetfighters, along with improved suspension systems, and better brakes.

Today, many bikers still customize their own bikes but for those who do not have the tools or know-how, there are many motorcycle shops that specialize in customizing bikes to suit their customers.

The Roar of an Engine

All motorcycles use internal combustion engines, which burn fuel to power the wheels of the bike. Most engines are described by how large they are, how many cylinders they have, and how much horsepower they are rated at.

The Two-Stroke Engine

Traditionally, there have been two basic types of motorcycle engines, the two-stroke and the four-stroke. Both types are internal combustion engines, and they operate on the same principles. Two-strokes are more lightweight, which makes them ideal for agile, off-road bikes, such as **motocross** bikes. Two-stroke engines endure a lot of wear and tear, causing them to break down more quickly than four-stroke engines, and they also release more polluting emissions into the air. Two-stroke engines used to power most bikes, but they are rarely seen on street bikes today.

The Four-Stroke Engine

Four-stroke engines produce power in four stages: intake, compression, power, and exhaust. At the intake stage, a piston moves down allowing air and fuel to enter the combustion chamber through the intake port. The intake valve then shuts, and the piston moves back up, compressing the air and fuel mixture within the chamber. The **spark plug** then fires, igniting the mixture, which produces a burst of energy that drives the piston back down. This is the power stage. Finally, the piston moves back to the top of the chamber, the exhaust valve opens, and the burnt fuel and air mixture is forced out through the exhaust outlet.

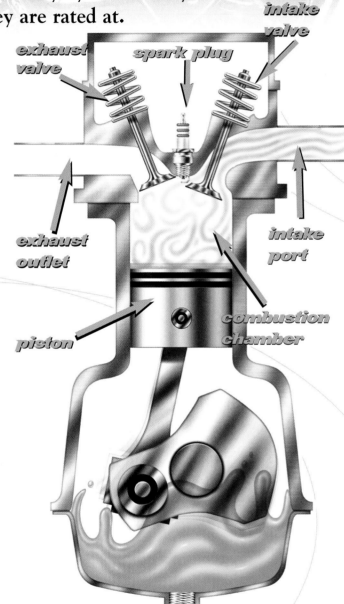

Most street bikes have four-stroke engines. The four stages of a four-stroke engine produce the energy that powers the motorcycle. The illustration above shows a cylinder, or chamber, in an internal combustion engine where the four-stroke cycle takes place.

Types of Four-Strokes

The cylinders of a four-stroke engine may be set up in different ways, and may also differ in the number of cylinders that power the engine. In general, engines run more smoothly if they have more cylinders, but adding cylinders also adds weight, which affects how well the bike handles. V set-ups have the cylinders arranged in a V-shape. V-twins have two cylinders while V-fours have four cylinders. Inline configurations have the cylinders arranged in a straight line, such as the popular inline-four, which has four cylinders. The opposed twin is a two-cylinder engine with cylinders that pump away from each other. It is sometimes called a "Boxer" because the cylinders look like fists punching the air.

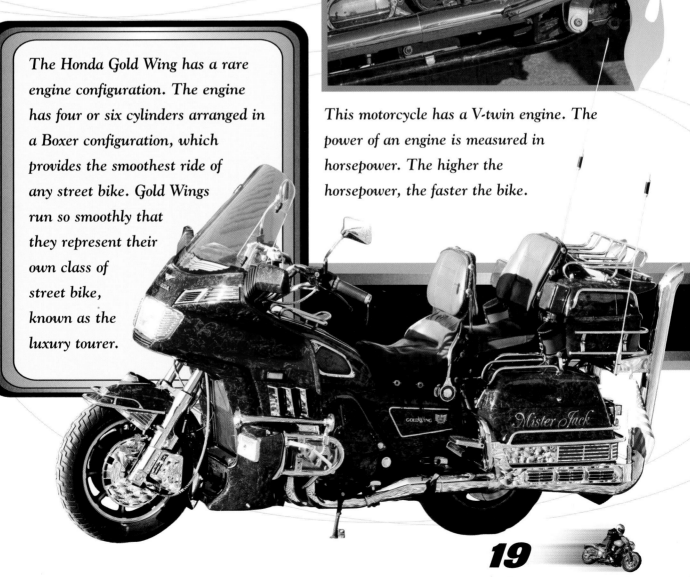

The Honda Gold Wing has a rare engine configuration. The engine has four or six cylinders arranged in a Boxer configuration, which provides the smoothest ride of any street bike. Gold Wings run so smoothly that they represent their own class of street bike, known as the luxury tourer.

This motorcycle has a V-twin engine. The power of an engine is measured in horsepower. The higher the horsepower, the faster the bike.

Anatomy of a Bike

There is much more to every street bike than fancy bodywork and a powerful engine. Motorcycles are complex machines with many different parts that coordinate to provide power.

The Engine

There are many different types of engines that power motorcycles today, but they all have two basic regions, known as the bottom and top ends. The bottom end includes parts that connect to the back wheel, creating forward motion. The top end is the upper portion of the engine, where internal combustion, or the four-stroke cycle takes place.

Throttle It

The throttle plays a big part in how the engine functions. The throttle is a twist grip found at the end of the right handlebar. It controls the bike's speed. Riders twist the grip toward them to increase the flow of fuel to the engine, which allows the bike to accelerate.

Frame

The frame of the bike is the basic body of the bike. It is the structure to which all of the other parts are attached, such as the wheels, suspension, and handlebars. Early motorcycles had crude frames made from metal tubes, but designers soon realized that a stiffer frame allows for better handling. Most bike frames for street riding are made of aluminum, steel, or a mixture of metals, known as an alloy.

Controlling the Bike

Primary and secondary controls help the rider handle the bike. Some of the primary controls are integrated into the handlebars, such as the throttle, clutch lever, and front brake lever. Unlike cars, motorcycles have two brake systems. The front brake is controlled by a lever on the right handle bar, while the back brake is operated using a lever next to the right footpeg. Secondary controls include the electric-starter button, turn signals, horn, headlight switch, and speedometer.

Clutch

The clutch allows riders to change gears by disengaging power between the **crankshaft** and the transmission. The first clutches were foot pedals, but were awkward to operate. Clutches are now levers on the handlebars, where riders can easily control them.

Transmission

The transmission is the system used to change gears. The gears alter the speed at which the engine pistons pump up and down, according to how quickly the rider wants the bike to go. After activating the clutch, riders step on a lever on the left side of the bike, engaging shifting forks, which activate the gears.

Suspension

The suspension is a system of springs, **shock absorbers**, and forks, or the metal tubes that connect the front of the bike frame to the front wheels. Suspensions help bikes handle so riders are not jostled with every bump in the road.

Wheels and Tires

A bike's wheels include the tires and the metal rims in the center of the tire. Motorcycles use radial tires, which are durable tires, reinforced with plies, or layers, of cords made of nylon. Radial tires are very strong and do not puncture easily.

The Gear

Most motorcyclists wear several pieces of gear in order to protect themselves from injury in the event of a crash. Some pieces of gear, such as the helmet, are mandatory in most countries.

Helmet

Helmets are the most important piece of gear that motorcyclists wear, and it is against the law not to wear them in Canada and most American states. Many riders who do not wear helmets do not survive accidents, and if they do, they often suffer head injuries or paralysis. The outer layer, or shell, of a helmet is made of hard fiberglass or plastic, and protects riders from impact. The lining of the helmet, often made of **polystyrene**, helps absorb impact. There is also foam padding inside, which makes the helmet more comfortable. A helmet needs to be replaced if the rider is in an accident, even if it is not cracked, because the materials weaken with every impact. Many helmets also come with face shields, which protect riders' faces from bugs and wind.

Gloves

Gloves are an important item of driving gear because they protect the rider's hands from being scraped, cut, or bruised in accidents. They also protect riders' hands from the weather. Proper gloves allow riders to grip the handlebars better than they would without gloves, giving riders more control. Most riding gloves are made from leather, with extra material covering the palms, fingers, and knuckles, as these parts are vulnerable to scraping in accidents. Gloves made from different materials are suited to different seasons, such as thinsulate gloves, which keep riders' hands warm in the winter.

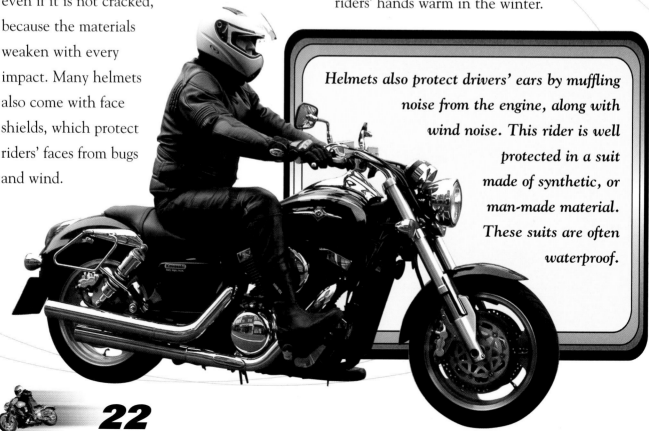

Helmets also protect drivers' ears by muffling noise from the engine, along with wind noise. This rider is well protected in a suit made of synthetic, or man-made material. These suits are often waterproof.

Layers

Aside from a helmet and gloves, it is recommended that motorcyclists wear long pants and jackets when riding, to protect their skin if they fall off their bikes. There are several different materials for riding gear, but leather is the most popular and most protective fabric. Motorcyclists may also choose synthetic suits, which, unlike leather, are usually water-resistant. In colder weather, motorcyclists need thermal layers, such as long underwear and balaclavas, which are head coverings riders wear under their helmets to keep their heads warm. Chaps are leather coverings that are worn over pants, to provide extra protection. They usually buckle around the waist, and often have zippers that run up the outside of the leg so they can be easily put on or taken off.

Riders should wear boots that come up over the ankle because they provide more protection.

Boots

Boots are important because they protect riders from burning themselves on their bikes' **tailpipes**. They also shield the rider from rocks and other debris that gets kicked up from the road. Boots should have excellent grip so riders' feet do not slip off the bike pegs or foot rests, and so the rider can support the bike when it is not moving.

Traditional riding gear is thought of as black leather jackets, vests, gloves, and chaps. This look was popular during the earlier days of motorcycling, and continues to be a major part of the street biker image.

23

Motorcycle Clubs

Motorcycle clubs are groups that motorcyclists join to meet other bikers. There are many different types of motorcycle clubs, but the members all have one thing in common: a love of riding.

Why Join a Club?

Most motorcyclists enjoy talking about the adventures they have had on the road, and motorcycle clubs are the perfect place to share these stories. Clubs are great places for motorcyclists to make new friends, and to get tips about the road or their bikes. Since many motorcyclists prefer fixing their own bikes rather than taking them to expensive garages, motorcycle clubs give riders a chance to swap mechanical information about their bikes. Motorcycle clubs also host several events for members, giving motorcyclists an opportunity to be part of a motorcycling community.

Club Activities

Motorcycle clubs offer a variety of activities for members. Organized rides are planned road tours in which the members of a club ride a specific route together. The members ride in one large cluster, making themselves even more visible to other motorists on the road. Some clubs also organize races and rallies for their members. Rallies are also activities that club members often attend together. Some clubs even produce their own magazines and newsletters, such as the Antique Motorcycle Club of America (A.M.C.A.), which publishes a quarterly magazine called The Antique Motorcycle.

The American Motorcyclist Association (AMA) was formed in 1924 and now has about 250,000 members. The AMA sponsors events all over the United States, including Daytona Bike Week, an event that brings thousands of bikers to Daytona, Florida, every year.

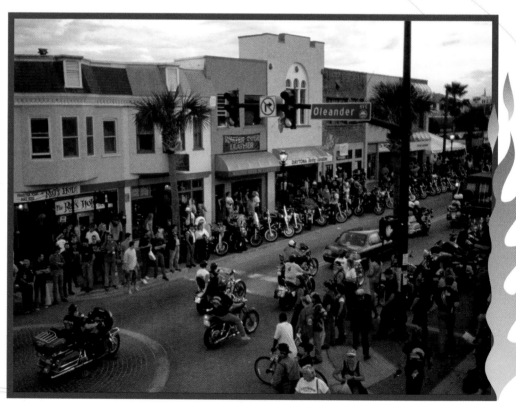

A Club for Everyone

There are many different types of motorcycle clubs, and new ones are being formed all of the time. Racing and sport bike clubs appeal to motorcyclists who enjoy racing, while touring clubs are for motorcyclists who enjoy traveling cross-country on their bikes. Make- or model-specific clubs are for motorcyclists who all have the same make of bike, such as BMW or Harley-Davidson. Other motorcycle clubs are gender-specific, such as Women On Wheels (WOW), and others focus on shared professions, such as the Blue Knights, whose members all work in law enforcement. Still other clubs form because of interests aside from motorcycling, such as the International Brotherhood of Motorcycle Campers, whose members enjoy camping while on the road rather than staying in hotels.

The Harley Owners Group, or HOG, is one of the best known make-specific motorcycle clubs in the United States.

Outlaws

The term "motorcycle gang" is often used to describe outlaw motorcycle clubs and are sometimes associated with illegal activities. Not all members of outlaw motorcycle clubs are criminals, but these clubs have carried reputations for breaking the law. Outlaw motorcycle clubs are usually portrayed in movies and television as organizations that attract dangerous people, and this stereotype has been difficult for other motorcycle clubs to live down. Members of these motorcycle clubs display their membership by wearing badges on the backs of their jackets, which display the gang's logo.

Some motorcycle gangs, such as the Hells Angels, have many chapters, or branches, throughout the United States and the world. These men are from the New York and Massachusetts chapters.

Rally Around

Motorcycle rallies are large events that attract hundreds to thousands of motorcyclists and people who are interested in motorcycle culture. There are many different rallies, and they attract bikers who have similar interests.

Rider Rallies

Motorcycle rallies are huge gatherings where motorcyclists can participate in races or other contests, purchase bike merchandise, such as leathers and other gear, attend or participate in stunt competitions, and most of all, show off their bikes to other riders. Rallies are sponsored by motorcycle clubs, and several of them also receive funding from the American Motorcyclist Association (AMA). Most rallies stretch out over several days, with some of them lasting a week or more.

Daytona Bike Week

The most well-known motorcycle rally, Daytona Bike Week, is held in Daytona, Florida, during the first week of March. This rally began as a racing event. Today, live bands are also featured, as well as bike shows for people to check out other bikes, especially ones that have been beautifully restored. Bike Week also includes fundraisers for charities, such as a blood drive held by the American Red Cross. Daytona is not considered a family event, as there are several components that are not appropriate for children.

Racing is still a big part of Daytona Bike Week. Aside from races for antique and classic bikes, the rally also hosts motocross, drag, and Superbike (below) racing. The Daytona 200 Superbike race is considered the most important event at the rally.

The Sturgis Motorcycle Rally in Sturgis, South Dakota, is a popular event, often attracting more than 500,000 motorcycle enthusiasts.

Americade

There are many other motorcycle rallies held throughout the year in the United States, and some of them are suitable for families to attend. Americade Motorcycle Rally is held at Lake George, New York, in early June. It is a rally for motorcyclists who enjoy and ride touring motorcycles. Americade attracts more than 50,000 bikers every year. The rally hosts a variety of events, including guided rides, cruises on sightseeing boats, and bike **demos** from some of the leading manufacturers of touring bikes, including Kawasaki, Triumph, Suzuki, Honda, BMW, and many more. Americade also features **trade shows** for motorcycle merchandise, as well as seminars on safe touring and motorcycle stunt shows.

Other Rallies

Some rallies are specific to motorcycle models, such as the Honda Hoot, held in Knoxville, Tennessee. The rally is for motorcyclists who ride or are interested in bikes made by Honda. The rally features organized rides, trade shows, and bike demos. BMW Motorcycle Owners of America hosts an annual rally for BMW motorcycle enthusiasts. Held in Burlington, Vermont, the rally features organized rides, trade shows, and seminars. Other rallies focus on motorcycling eras, such as Vintage Motorcycle Days, organized by the AMA, which are held in Ohio each July. Most enthusiasts agree that a vintage motorcycle is any bike made between the years of 1915 and 1930. Vintage Motorcycle Days features stunt shows, demos, exhibits, and races.

Bike Safety

There is more to motorcycling than wearing the appropriate gear. Motorcyclists must obey the rules of the road and drive responsibly. Motorcyclists should ride bikes that are compatible, or suited, with their capabilities.

Staying Safe

Motorcycles are fun to learn about and ride, but they can be dangerous. They do not protect drivers in the same way that cars do, because there is no outer shell or body to provide a barrier between the rider and the road, or other vehicles. Motorcycle crashes often result in severe injuries, or even fatalities, so it is important for riders to exercise caution on the road. The Motorcycle Safety Foundation (MSF) stresses five major objectives that should become all riders' priorities. They include obtaining the proper training and licensing, wearing the appropriate gear, riding without the influence of alcohol, not riding recklessly, and knowing that motorcycling is a lifelong learning experience.

A Foundation of Safety

The Motorcycle Safety Foundation was founded in 1973. It is a **not-for-profit** organization that trains motorcyclists in the United States to ride their bikes safely. MSF is funded by motorcycle manufacturers, including Harley-Davidson, BMW, Honda, Kawasaki, Triumph, Yamaha, and others. MSF works with the National Highway Traffic Safety Administration (NHTSA), a government agency, to develop regulations, or rules, that will help keep motorcyclists safe. They also work with the American government to promote public awareness of motorcycle safety and motorcyclists' rights on the road. Many other countries have similar motorcycle safety organizations that train motorcyclists to handle bikes safely.

In 2006, Honda became the first manufacturer to install airbags in motorcycles. Airbags cushion riders when they hit objects head on, reducing the chance of injury.

Preparing for the Road

There is a lot more to learning how to ride than figuring out how to turn a key in the ignition. Riding motorcycles is a complicated process. Riders not only have to learn how to operate a bike, but how to do so without endangering other motorists on the road, as well as cyclists and pedestrians. Motorcyclists must follow the laws of the road. The Motorcycle Safety Foundation offers courses to beginner and advanced motorcyclists. These courses are offered all over the United States, and they are built to educate motorcyclists on the rules of the road, as well as how to handle different styles of bikes.

License to Ride

It is illegal to drive a motorcycle without a valid motorcycle license. Most states in the United States have similar steps and standards for obtaining a motorcycle license. In general, people who want a motorcycle license must be at least 16 years old. They then pay a fee, complete an application, and write a test on rules of the road, as they apply to motorcyclists. Applicants who pass the test are granted a motorcycle permit, which allows the rider to drive a bike with certain restrictions. Common restrictions of a permit are that the rider must drive only during daylight, and with no passengers. Licenses are granted only to people who successfully complete a road test. During a road test, an examiner studies how well the rider controls a bike. Most states also require riders to complete a training course through the MSF before receiving a motorcycle license.

Rider safety courses teach people how to ride motorcycles safely in different types of weather and on a variety of terrains, including highways, dirt roads, and off-road.

Behind the Machines

People who build motorcycles have imagination and vision. It is because of these inspired individuals that motorcycles have survived bad press and remain popular today.

Harley and Davidson

William S. Harley was born in Milwaukee, Wisconsin, on December 29, 1880. He started working in a bicycle factory when he was 15 years old. It was there that he met up with childhood friend, Arthur Davidson, who was one year older than William. It was not long before the two friends began trying to build motorized bikes. They attached small gasoline-powered engines to their bikes, and by 1904, the pair had built their first motorcycle. Two of Arthur's brothers, William and Walter Davidson, joined the operation, and by 1907, the Harley-Davidson Motor Company became a registered **trademark**. The company's motorcycles were used for racing, but they now produce mostly street bikes.

William Harley and William Davidson used a motorcycle and sidecar made by Harley-Davidson to go on fishing trips.

Willie G.

William G. Davidson is a big name in the motorcycle world. He is the grandson of William Davidson, and is considered to be one of the first motorcycle customizers. Known as "Willie G.," he began his design career in the styling department of Harley-Davidson. Three of his designs, the Super Glide of 1971, the Low Rider of 1977, and the Wide Glide of 1980, have earned him an excellent reputation. Willie G. is now the Vice President of Styling at Harley-Davidson, and the head of the Willie G. Davidson Product Development Center, which designs and tests motorcycles for performance and safety. Willie G. continues to design bikes and is often seen promoting Harley-Davidson bikes at rallies.

Willie G. was inducted into the American Motorcycle Association Hall of Fame in 1999.

Arlen Ness

Arlen Ness is another huge name in motorcycle customizing. He began his career in 1967, when he bought his first Harley. Ness modified his bike by stripping it of parts he thought unnecessary, and re-painting it. Ness entered the bike into a custom show, which he won, and immediately began getting requests from other bikers to customize their bikes. Ness now runs a customizing shop in Dublin, California. Arlen Ness Motorcycles debuted three new models at the Sturgis Rally of 2005, and all three were well received. The Low Liner is a long, lean, sleek-looking bike with extended forks and low handlebars. The Speed Liner is a taller bike with chrome detailing and extended forks. The High Liner is a chopper with extremely high forks and a colorful paint job.

Arlen Ness' motto is "Always innovate, never imitate," which holds true for all his custom bike designs.

Jesse James

Customizing motorcycles continues to be a popular trend today, but where people used to customize their bikes themselves, the most outrageous customized bikes come from specialty shops. Jesse James, owner of West Coast Choppers in Long Beach, California, is one of the most well-known bike customizers. Every styling element of each bike is personalized to suit a customer's taste. Many of James' custom bikes feature extended forks, similar to the first choppers, but they also include colorful, individual paint jobs, and chrome detailing. Each bike features different styles of handlebars, seating, and wheels. No two bikes are the same at West Coast Choppers.

Jesse James' motorcycles have appeared on his television series, "Monster Garage."

Glossary

chrome A shiny metal finish

crankshaft The device that spins to make pistons in the engine pump up and down

cruise control A device that keeps a bike traveling at a pre-determined speed

demo Shows that portray products' characteristics or performance capabilities

economical Something that provides good performance for low cost

economy A system that brings money into a region, and includes making and selling goods

emissions Exhaust fumes that rise into the air

endurance The ability to last a long time

enthusiasts People who are passionate about something

fuel-efficient Burning as little fuel as possible to get from place to place

handle The way a bike takes corners and bumps; it relates to how well a driver can control a bike

insurance companies Businesses that bikers pay fees to for protection from costs to repair their bikes if they are damaged in accidents or stolen

internal combustion The process of igniting a fuel to provide power

matte A dull, non-shiny finish

motocross A type of race run on off-road tracks

not-for-profit A company or organization that receives little or no money for what they do; these organizations are run largely by volunteers

outlaws People who are known to break the law

polystyrene A lightweight foamy material

postwar boom A period of wealth following war

revolutionized Made large changes to something

shock absorbers Springs that help cushion a rider from bumps in the road

spark plug A device that ignites the fuel-air mixture in the combustion chambers of an engine

steam engine An engine that uses steam from boiling water to provide power

suspension The system of shock absorbers that protect a biker from jostling when riding over bumpy terrain

tailpipe The metal pipe that allows used up gases to exit bike engines

trademark A name or symbol representing a company, and can only be used by that company

trade shows Places people go to look at bikes, products, and gear from motorcycle manufacturers

World War II A major global conflict that took place from 1939 to 1945

Index

Printed in the U.S.A.